This book belongs to:

D1403505

Go See
≡ THE ≡
WORLD!

I ♥ travel

Location: _____

_____

_____

DATE: _____

WEATHER:

TODAYS ACTIVITY: _____

THE MOST INTERESTING I SAW: _____

TODAY I ATE: _____

TODAY I LEARNED: _____

Sketch what you saw:

RATE YOUR DAY:

TODAY'S FAVORITE MEMORY:

TODAY I AM GRATEFUL FOR:

Location: _____ DATE: _____

```
        N
   W    +    E
        S
```
_____

_____

WEATHER:

☀ ⛅ ☁ 🌧

TODAYS ACTIVITY:

_____

_____

_____

_____

THE MOST INTERESTING I SAW:

_____

_____

_____

TODAY I ATE:

_____

_____

_____

TODAY I LEARNED:

_____

_____

_____

_____

Sketch what you saw:

RATE YOUR DAY:

TODAY'S FAVORITE MEMORY:

TODAY I AM GRATEFUL FOR:

Location:

DATE:

WEATHER:

TODAYS ACTIVITY:

- -

THE MOST INTERESTING I SAW:

- -

TODAY I ATE:

- -

TODAY I LEARNED:

Sketch what you saw:

RATE YOUR DAY:

TODAY'S FAVORITE MEMORY:

TODAY I AM GRATEFUL FOR:

Location:

DATE:

WEATHER:

N
W E
S

TODAYS ACTIVITY:

THE MOST INTERESTING I SAW:

TODAY I ATE:

TODAY I LEARNED:

Sketch what you saw:

RATE YOUR DAY:

TODAY'S FAVORITE MEMORY:

TODAY I AM GRATEFUL FOR:

Location: _____

DATE: _____

N
W — E
S

WEATHER:

TODAYS ACTIVITY:
_____
_____
_____
_____
_____
_____

THE MOST INTERESTING I SAW:
_____
_____
_____

TODAY I ATE:
_____
_____
_____

TODAY I LEARNED:
_____
_____
_____
_____
_____

Sketch what you saw:

RATE YOUR DAY:

TODAY'S FAVORITE MEMORY:

TODAY I AM GRATEFUL FOR:

Location: _____

DATE: _____

_____

_____

WEATHER:

N
W — E
S

TODAYS ACTIVITY:

_____

_____

_____

_____

_____

THE MOST INTERESTING I SAW:

_____

_____

_____

TODAY I ATE:

_____

_____

_____

TODAY I LEARNED:

_____

_____

_____

_____

Sketch what you saw:

RATE YOUR DAY:

TODAY'S FAVORITE MEMORY:

TODAY I AM GRATEFUL FOR:

Location:

DATE:

N
W — E
S

WEATHER:

• •

TODAYS ACTIVITY:

- -

THE MOST INTERESTING I SAW:

- -

TODAY I ATE:

- -

TODAY I LEARNED:

Sketch what you saw:

RATE YOUR DAY:

TODAY'S FAVORITE MEMORY:

TODAY I AM GRATEFUL FOR:

Location:

DATE: _____

WEATHER:

TODAYS ACTIVITY:

THE MOST INTERESTING I SAW:

TODAY I ATE:

TODAY I LEARNED:

Sketch what you saw:

RATE YOUR DAY:

TODAY'S FAVORITE MEMORY:

TODAY I AM GRATEFUL FOR:

Location: _____

N
W E
S

WEATHER:

TODAYS ACTIVITY: _____

THE MOST INTERESTING I SAW: _____

TODAY I ATE: _____

TODAY I LEARNED: _____

Sketch what you saw:

RATE YOUR DAY:

TODAY'S FAVORITE MEMORY:

TODAY I AM GRATEFUL FOR:

Location: _____

DATE: _____

N
W — E _____
S _____

WEATHER:

TODAYS ACTIVITY: _____
_____
_____
_____
_____
_____

THE MOST INTERESTING I SAW: _____
_____
_____

TODAY I ATE: _____
_____
_____

TODAY I LEARNED: _____
_____
_____
_____
_____

Sketch what you saw:

RATE YOUR DAY:

TODAY'S FAVORITE MEMORY:

TODAY I AM GRATEFUL FOR:

Location: _____

N
W — E
S

WEATHER:

TODAYS ACTIVITY: _____
_____
_____
_____
_____

THE MOST INTERESTING I SAW: _____
_____
_____
_____

TODAY I ATE: _____
_____
_____
_____

TODAY I LEARNED: _____
_____
_____
_____
_____

Sketch what you saw:

RATE YOUR DAY:

TODAY'S FAVORITE MEMORY:

TODAY I AM GRATEFUL FOR:

Location: _____

DATE: _____

WEATHER:

_____

_____

TODAYS ACTIVITY: _____
_____
_____
_____
_____
_____

THE MOST INTERESTING I SAW: _____
_____
_____

TODAY I ATE: _____
_____
_____

TODAY I LEARNED: _____
_____
_____
_____
_____

Sketch what you saw:

RATE YOUR DAY:

TODAY'S FAVORITE MEMORY:

TODAY I AM GRATEFUL FOR:

Location: _____

DATE: _____

N
W — E
S

WEATHER:

TODAYS ACTIVITY: _____
_____
_____
_____
_____

THE MOST INTERESTING I SAW: _____
_____
_____
_____

TODAY I ATE: _____
_____
_____
_____

TODAY I LEARNED: _____
_____
_____
_____
_____

Sketch what you saw:

RATE YOUR DAY:

TODAY'S FAVORITE MEMORY:

TODAY I AM GRATEFUL FOR:

Location:

DATE:

N
W—E
S

WEATHER:

TODAYS ACTIVITY:

THE MOST INTERESTING I SAW:

TODAY I ATE:

TODAY I LEARNED:

Sketch what you saw:

RATE YOUR DAY:

TODAY'S FAVORITE MEMORY:

TODAY I AM GRATEFUL FOR:

Location:

DATE:

WEATHER:

N
W · E
S

TODAYS ACTIVITY:

THE MOST INTERESTING I SAW:

TODAY I ATE:

TODAY I LEARNED:

Sketch what you saw:

RATE YOUR DAY:

TODAY'S FAVORITE MEMORY:

TODAY I AM GRATEFUL FOR:

Location: _____

DATE: _____

```
      N
  W ──┼── E
      S
```

WEATHER:

_____
_____
_____

TODAYS ACTIVITY:
_____
_____
_____
_____
_____
_____

- - - - - - - - - - - - - - - - -

THE MOST INTERESTING I SAW:
_____
_____
_____

- - - - - - - - - - - - - - - - -

TODAY I ATE:
_____
_____
_____
_____

- - - - - - - - - - - - - - - - -

TODAY I LEARNED:
_____
_____
_____
_____
_____
_____

Sketch what you saw:

RATE YOUR DAY:

TODAY'S FAVORITE MEMORY:

TODAY I AM GRATEFUL FOR:

Location:

DATE:

WEATHER:

TODAYS ACTIVITY:

THE MOST INTERESTING I SAW:

TODAY I ATE:

TODAY I LEARNED:

Sketch what you saw:

RATE YOUR DAY:

TODAY'S FAVORITE MEMORY:

TODAY I AM GRATEFUL FOR:

Location:

DATE:

N
W E
S

WEATHER:

TODAYS ACTIVITY:

THE MOST INTERESTING I SAW:

TODAY I ATE:

TODAY I LEARNED:

Sketch what you saw:

RATE YOUR DAY:

TODAY'S FAVORITE MEMORY:

TODAY I AM GRATEFUL FOR:

Location:

DATE:

WEATHER:

TODAYS ACTIVITY:

THE MOST INTERESTING I SAW:

TODAY I ATE:

TODAY I LEARNED:

Sketch what you saw:

RATE YOUR DAY:

TODAY'S FAVORITE MEMORY:

TODAY I AM GRATEFUL FOR:

Location: _____

DATE: _____

N / W—E / S

WEATHER:

☀ ⛅ ☁ 🌧

TODAYS ACTIVITY: _____

_____
_____
_____
_____
_____

THE MOST INTERESTING I SAW: _____

_____
_____
_____

TODAY I ATE: _____

_____
_____
_____

TODAY I LEARNED: _____

_____
_____
_____
_____
_____

Sketch what you saw:

RATE YOUR DAY:

TODAY'S FAVORITE MEMORY:

TODAY I AM GRATEFUL FOR:

Location:

DATE:

WEATHER:

TODAYS ACTIVITY:

THE MOST INTERESTING I SAW:

TODAY I ATE:

TODAY I LEARNED:

Sketch what you saw:

RATE YOUR DAY:

TODAY'S FAVORITE MEMORY: _____

TODAY I AM GRATEFUL FOR: _____

Location: _____

DATE: _____

N
W — E
S

WEATHER:

TODAYS ACTIVITY: _____

_____

_____

_____

_____

_____

THE MOST INTERESTING I SAW: _____

_____

_____

_____

TODAY I ATE: _____

_____

_____

_____

TODAY I LEARNED: _____

_____

_____

_____

_____

Sketch what you saw:

RATE YOUR DAY:

TODAY'S FAVORITE MEMORY:

TODAY I AM GRATEFUL FOR:

Location: _____

DATE: _____

N
W ⊹ E
S

_____
_____
_____

WEATHER:

☀ ⛅ ☁ 🌧

TODAYS ACTIVITY: _____

THE MOST INTERESTING I SAW: _____

TODAY I ATE: _____

TODAY I LEARNED: _____

Sketch what you saw:

RATE YOUR DAY:

TODAY'S FAVORITE MEMORY:

TODAY I AM GRATEFUL FOR:

Location:

DATE:

N
W E
S

WEATHER:

TODAYS ACTIVITY:

THE MOST INTERESTING I SAW:

TODAY I ATE:

TODAY I LEARNED:

Sketch what you saw:

RATE YOUR DAY:

TODAY'S FAVORITE MEMORY:

TODAY I AM GRATEFUL FOR:

Location:

DATE:

WEATHER:

N
W E
S

TODAYS ACTIVITY:

THE MOST INTERESTING I SAW:

TODAY I ATE:

TODAY I LEARNED:

Sketch what you saw:

RATE YOUR DAY:

TODAY'S FAVORITE MEMORY:

TODAY I AM GRATEFUL FOR:

Location: _____

DATE: _____

N
W — E
S

WEATHER:

TODAYS ACTIVITY: _____

THE MOST INTERESTING I SAW: _____

TODAY I ATE: _____

TODAY I LEARNED: _____

Sketch what you saw:

RATE YOUR DAY:

TODAY'S FAVORITE MEMORY:

TODAY I AM GRATEFUL FOR:

Location:

DATE:

N

W — E

S

WEATHER:

TODAYS ACTIVITY:

THE MOST INTERESTING I SAW:

TODAY I ATE:

TODAY I LEARNED:

Sketch what you saw:

RATE YOUR DAY:

TODAY'S FAVORITE MEMORY:

TODAY I AM GRATEFUL FOR:

Location: _____

DATE: _____

N
W ⊕ E
S

WEATHER:

TODAYS ACTIVITY: _____

_____

_____

_____

THE MOST INTERESTING I SAW: _____

_____

_____

TODAY I ATE: _____

_____

_____

TODAY I LEARNED: _____

_____

_____

_____

Sketch what you saw:

RATE YOUR DAY:

TODAY'S FAVORITE MEMORY:

TODAY I AM GRATEFUL FOR:

Location: _____

DATE: _____

```
        N
    W ⟡ E
        S
```
_____

_____

WEATHER:

☀ ⛅ ☁ 🌧

●●●●●●●●●●●●●●●●●●●●●●●●●●●●●●●●

TODAYS ACTIVITY: _____

_____

_____

_____

_____

- - - - - - - - - - - - - -

THE MOST INTERESTING I SAW: _____

_____

_____

- - - - - - - - - - - - - -

TODAY I ATE: _____

_____

_____

- - - - - - - - - - - - - -

TODAY I LEARNED: _____

_____

_____

_____

Sketch what you saw:

RATE YOUR DAY:

TODAY'S FAVORITE MEMORY:

TODAY I AM GRATEFUL FOR:

Location: _____

N
W E
S

WEATHER:

TODAYS ACTIVITY: _____

THE MOST INTERESTING I SAW: _____

TODAY I ATE: _____

TODAY I LEARNED: _____

Sketch what you saw:

RATE YOUR DAY:

TODAY'S FAVORITE MEMORY:

TODAY I AM GRATEFUL FOR:

Location:

DATE: _____

WEATHER:

N
W — E
S

TODAYS ACTIVITY: _____

_____

_____

_____

_____

_____

THE MOST INTERESTING I SAW: _____

_____

_____

_____

TODAY I ATE: _____

_____

_____

_____

TODAY I LEARNED: _____

_____

_____

_____

_____

_____

Sketch what you saw:

RATE YOUR DAY:

TODAY'S FAVORITE MEMORY:

TODAY I AM GRATEFUL FOR:

Location:

DATE:

N
W E
S

WEATHER:

TODAYS ACTIVITY:

THE MOST INTERESTING I SAW:

TODAY I ATE:

TODAY I LEARNED:

Sketch what you saw:

RATE YOUR DAY:

TODAY'S FAVORITE MEMORY:

TODAY I AM GRATEFUL FOR:

Location: _____

DATE: _____

N
W · E
S

WEATHER: ☀ ⛅ ☁ 🌧

TODAYS ACTIVITY: _____
_____
_____
_____
_____
_____

THE MOST INTERESTING I SAW: _____
_____
_____

TODAY I ATE: _____
_____
_____

TODAY I LEARNED: _____
_____
_____
_____
_____

Sketch what you saw:

RATE YOUR DAY:

TODAY'S FAVORITE MEMORY:

TODAY I AM GRATEFUL FOR:

Location: _____

DATE: _____

N
W E
S

WEATHER:

TODAYS ACTIVITY: _____

_____

_____

_____

_____

_____

THE MOST INTERESTING I SAW: _____

_____

_____

_____

TODAY I ATE: _____

_____

_____

_____

TODAY I LEARNED: _____

_____

_____

_____

_____

Sketch what you saw:

RATE YOUR DAY:

TODAY'S FAVORITE MEMORY:

TODAY I AM GRATEFUL FOR:

Location:

DATE:

N
W E
S

WEATHER:

TODAYS ACTIVITY:

THE MOST INTERESTING I SAW:

TODAY I ATE:

TODAY I LEARNED:

Sketch what you saw:

RATE YOUR DAY:

TODAY'S FAVORITE MEMORY:

TODAY I AM GRATEFUL FOR:

Location: _____

DATE: _____

WEATHER:

☀ ⛅ ☁ 🌧

TODAYS ACTIVITY: _____

_____

_____

_____

_____

THE MOST INTERESTING I SAW: _____

_____

_____

_____

TODAY I ATE: _____

_____

_____

TODAY I LEARNED: _____

_____

_____

_____

_____

Sketch what you saw:

RATE YOUR DAY:

TODAY'S FAVORITE MEMORY:

TODAY I AM GRATEFUL FOR:

Location:

DATE:

WEATHER:

N
W E
S

TODAYS ACTIVITY:

THE MOST INTERESTING I SAW:

TODAY I ATE:

TODAY I LEARNED:

Sketch what you saw:

RATE YOUR DAY:

TODAY'S FAVORITE MEMORY:

TODAY I AM GRATEFUL FOR:

Location: _____

DATE: _____

N
W ✦ E
S

WEATHER: _____

TODAYS ACTIVITY: _____

THE MOST INTERESTING I SAW: _____

TODAY I ATE: _____

TODAY I LEARNED: _____

Sketch what you saw:

RATE YOUR DAY: 😎 😃 🙂 😐 😵

TODAY'S FAVORITE MEMORY:

TODAY I AM GRATEFUL FOR:

Location: _____

DATE: _____

WEATHER:

TODAYS ACTIVITY: _____
_____
_____
_____
_____
_____
_____

THE MOST INTERESTING I SAW: _____
_____
_____
_____

TODAY I ATE: _____
_____
_____
_____

TODAY I LEARNED: _____
_____
_____
_____
_____
_____
_____

Sketch what you saw:

RATE YOUR DAY:

TODAY'S FAVORITE MEMORY:

TODAY I AM GRATEFUL FOR:

Location:

DATE:

WEATHER:

TODAYS ACTIVITY:

THE MOST INTERESTING I SAW:

TODAY I ATE:

TODAY I LEARNED:

Sketch what you saw:

RATE YOUR DAY:

TODAY'S FAVORITE MEMORY:

TODAY I AM GRATEFUL FOR:

Location: _____

_____

_____

N
W — E
S

WEATHER:

TODAYS ACTIVITY: _____
_____
_____
_____
_____
_____

THE MOST INTERESTING I SAW: _____
_____
_____
_____

TODAY I ATE: _____
_____
_____
_____

TODAY I LEARNED: _____
_____
_____
_____
_____
_____

Sketch what you saw:

RATE YOUR DAY:

TODAY'S FAVORITE MEMORY:

TODAY I AM GRATEFUL FOR:

Location:

DATE:

WEATHER:

N
W E
S

TODAYS ACTIVITY:

THE MOST INTERESTING I SAW:

TODAY I ATE:

TODAY I LEARNED:

Sketch what you saw:

RATE YOUR DAY:

ODAY'S FAVORITE MEMORY:

ODAY I AM GRATEFUL FOR:

Location: _____

N
W — E
S

DATE: _____

WEATHER:

TODAYS ACTIVITY: _____
_____
_____
_____
_____
_____

THE MOST INTERESTING I SAW: _____
_____
_____
_____

TODAY I ATE: _____
_____
_____

TODAY I LEARNED: _____
_____
_____
_____
_____

Sketch what you saw:

RATE YOUR DAY:

TODAY'S FAVORITE MEMORY:

TODAY I AM GRATEFUL FOR:

Location:

DATE:

WEATHER:

N
W · E
S

TODAYS ACTIVITY:

THE MOST INTERESTING I SAW:

TODAY I ATE:

TODAY I LEARNED:

Sketch what you saw:

RATE YOUR DAY:

TODAY'S FAVORITE MEMORY:

TODAY I AM GRATEFUL FOR:

Location: _____

DATE: _____

N
W — E
S

WEATHER:

TODAYS ACTIVITY: _____

- - - - - - - - - - - - - - - - - - - -

THE MOST INTERESTING I SAW: _____

- - - - - - - - - - - - - - - - - - - -

TODAY I ATE: _____

- - - - - - - - - - - - - - - - - - - -

TODAY I LEARNED: _____

Sketch what you saw:

RATE YOUR DAY:

TODAY'S FAVORITE MEMORY:

TODAY I AM GRATEFUL FOR:

Location: _____

DATE: _____

WEATHER:

N
W — E
S

TODAYS ACTIVITY: _____

THE MOST INTERESTING I SAW: _____

TODAY I ATE: _____

TODAY I LEARNED: _____

Sketch what you saw:

RATE YOUR DAY:

TODAY'S FAVORITE MEMORY:

TODAY I AM GRATEFUL FOR:

Location: _____

DATE: _____

WEATHER:

TODAYS ACTIVITY: _____

THE MOST INTERESTING I SAW: _____

TODAY I ATE: _____

TODAY I LEARNED: _____

Sketch what you saw:

RATE YOUR DAY:

TODAY'S FAVORITE MEMORY:

TODAY I AM GRATEFUL FOR:

Location:

DATE: _____

WEATHER:

N
W — E
S

TODAYS ACTIVITY: _____

THE MOST INTERESTING I SAW: _____

TODAY I ATE: _____

TODAY I LEARNED: _____

Sketch what you saw:

RATE YOUR DAY:

TODAY'S FAVORITE MEMORY:

TODAY I AM GRATEFUL FOR:

Location: _____

DATE: _____

WEATHER:

TODAYS ACTIVITY: _____

THE MOST INTERESTING I SAW: _____

TODAY I ATE: _____

TODAY I LEARNED: _____

Sketch what you saw:

RATE YOUR DAY:

TODAY'S FAVORITE MEMORY:

TODAY I AM GRATEFUL FOR:

Location: _____

DATE: _____

WEATHER:

TODAYS ACTIVITY: _____

_____

_____

_____

_____

THE MOST INTERESTING I SAW: _____

_____

_____

TODAY I ATE: _____

_____

_____

TODAY I LEARNED: _____

_____

_____

_____

_____

Sketch what you saw:

RATE YOUR DAY:

TODAY'S FAVORITE MEMORY:

TODAY I AM GRATEFUL FOR:

Location: _____

DATE: _____

N
W   E
S

WEATHER:

TODAYS ACTIVITY: _____
_____
_____
_____
_____
_____

THE MOST INTERESTING I SAW: _____
_____
_____

TODAY I ATE: _____
_____
_____

TODAY I LEARNED: _____
_____
_____
_____

Sketch what you saw:

RATE YOUR DAY:

TODAY'S FAVORITE MEMORY:

TODAY I AM GRATEFUL FOR:

Location: _____

N
W — E
S

WEATHER:

TODAYS ACTIVITY: _____
_____
_____
_____
_____
_____

THE MOST INTERESTING I SAW: _____
_____
_____
_____

TODAY I ATE: _____
_____
_____
_____

TODAY I LEARNED: _____
_____
_____
_____
_____
_____

Sketch what you saw:

RATE YOUR DAY:

TODAY'S FAVORITE MEMORY:

TODAY I AM GRATEFUL FOR:

Location: _____ DATE: _____

N
W ⊕ E   WEATHER: ☀ ⛅ ☁ 🌧
S
_____
_____

•••

TODAYS ACTIVITY: _____
_____
_____
_____
_____
_____

THE MOST INTERESTING I SAW: _____
_____
_____

TODAY I ATE: _____
_____
_____

TODAY I LEARNED: _____
_____
_____
_____
_____

Sketch what you saw:

RATE YOUR DAY:

TODAY'S FAVORITE MEMORY:

TODAY I AM GRATEFUL FOR:

Location: _____   DATE: _____

WEATHER:

N
W   E
S
_____

TODAYS ACTIVITY: _____

THE MOST INTERESTING I SAW: _____

TODAY I ATE: _____

TODAY I LEARNED: _____

Sketch what you saw:

RATE YOUR DAY:

TODAY'S FAVORITE MEMORY:

TODAY I AM GRATEFUL FOR:

Location: _____

_____

DATE: _____

WEATHER:

N
W——E
S

TODAYS ACTIVITY: _____

THE MOST INTERESTING I SAW: _____

TODAY I ATE: _____

TODAY I LEARNED: _____

Sketch what you saw:

RATE YOUR DAY:

TODAY'S FAVORITE MEMORY:

TODAY I AM GRATEFUL FOR:

Made in the USA
Coppell, TX
26 April 2022

77043421R00063